DO ANTS GET LOST?

Learning about Animal Communication with

THE GARBAGE GANG

by Thomas Kingsley Troupe   Illustrated by Derek Toye

PICTURE WINDOW BOOKS
a capstone imprint

MEET THE GARBAGE GANG:

SAM HAMMWICH

Sam is a once-delicious sandwich that has a bit of lettuce and tomato. He is usually crabby and a bit of a loudmouth.

GORDY

Gordy is a small rhino who wears an eyepatch even though he doesn't need one. He lives in the city dump. His friends don't visit him in the smelly dump, so Gordy created his own friends—the Garbage Gang!

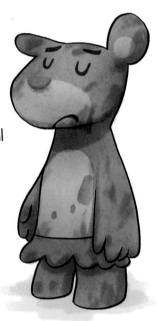

SOGGY

Soggy is a stuffed bear from a carnival game. She fell into a puddle of dumpster juice and has never been the same.

RICK

Rick is a brick. He is terrified of bugs, especially bees, which is odd . . . since he's a brick.

CANN-DEE

Cann-Dee is a robot made of aluminum cans. She can pull random facts out of thin air.

MR. FRIGID

Mr. Frigid is a huge refrigerator that sprouted arms and legs. He doesn't say much, but he's super strong.

It's weird, isn't it Gordy? They're coming all this way to get our food. That grass must seem like a jungle!

It makes me wonder— do ants get lost?

Hey up there! Do you have a question about ants?

9

I know you don't care, Gordy, but I'm made of food. Those creepy-crawlies would love to take a piece outta me!

And I just don't like bugs!

Calm down, guys. We mostly go after the crumbs. Also, I don't like eating ham sandwiches or bricks.

Does the stink trail you guys leave smell bad?

Not to us. But ants aren't the only creatures to use scent to communicate.

Well, they also bark, use tail movements, and show their teeth. So they communicate in lots of ways.

15

Looks like it's time to head home. You know your way, Alice?

Are you kidding? We left a really good scent trail. Getting home will be a piece of cake. See you later, Garbage Gang!

Goodbye, Alice! Enjoy those crumbs!

Look! The dogs are heading home too.

We go home now?

Yes, and it'll be easy to find our home. We just head toward the stinkiest place in town!

Glossary

communicate—to pass along thoughts, feelings, or ideas

feces—another word for poop

scent glands—small sacs that hold scent fluids

territory—an area of land that an animal claims as its own to live in

threatened—to feel as though there is danger present

urine—pee

vocal—relating to voice

You're looking up words? That's one smart move, kid!

Read More

Eschbach, Andrea. *How to Speak "Horse": A Horse-Crazy Kid's Guide to Reading Body Language and "Talking Back."* North Pomfret, Vt.: Trafalgar Square Books, 2012.

Newman, Aline Alexander. *How to Speak Dog: A Guide to Decoding Dog Language.* Washington, D.C.: National Geographic, 2013.

Townsend, John. *Amazing Animal Communicators.* Animal Superpowers. Chicago: Raintree, 2013.

Incoming data suggests that books don't stink.

Critical Thinking Using the Common Core

1. What are some animals that use scent to communicate? How do they do so? (Key Ideas and Details)

2. Name some ways people communicate. Are some of the ways similar to the ways other animals communicate? (Integration of Knowedge and Ideas)

Index

Internet Sites

FactHound offers a safe, fun way to find Internet sites related to this book. All of the sites on FactHound have been researched by our staff.

Here's all you do:

Visit www.facthound.com

Type in this code: 9781479554782

Super-cool stuff! Check out projects, games and lots more at www.capstonekids.com

Thanks to our advisers for their expertise, research, and advice:
Christopher T. Ruhland, PhD
Professor of Biological Sciences
Department of Biology
Minnesota State University, Mankato

Terry Flaherty, PhD, Professor of English
Minnesota State University, Mankato

Editor: Shelly Lyons
Designer: Lori Bye
Art Director: Nathan Gassman
Production Specialist: Gene Bentdahl
The illustrations in this book were created digitally
Picture Window Books are published by Capstone,
1710 Roe Crest Drive, North Mankato, Minnesota 56003
www.capstonepub.com

Library of Congress Cataloging-in-Publication Data
Troupe, Thomas Kingsley, author.
Do ants get lost? : learning about animal communication with the Garbage Gang / by Thomas Kingsley Troupe ; illustrated by Derek Toye.
pages cm. — (Nonfiction picture books. The Garbage Gang's super science questions)
Summary: "Humorous text and characters teach kids all about scent marking and animal communication"— Provided by publisher.
Audience: Ages 5-7.
Audience: K to grade 3.
Includes bibliographical references and index.
ISBN 978-1-4795-5478-2 (library binding)
ISBN 978-1-4795-5486-7 (eBook PDF)
1. Animal communication—Juvenile literature. 2. Ants—Juvenile literature. I. Toye, Derek, illustrator. II. Title.
QL776.T76 2015
591.59—dc23   2014002361

Printed in the United States of America in North Mankato, Minnesota.
032014   008087CGF14

Look for all the books in the series:

DO ANTS GET LOST? Learning about Animal Communication with **THE GARBAGE GANG**

DO BEES POOP? Learning about Living and Nonliving Things with **THE GARBAGE GANG**

WHY DO DEAD FISH FLOAT? Learning about Matter with **THE GARBAGE GANG**

WHY DOES MY BODY MAKE BUBBLES? Learning about the Digestive System with **THE GARBAGE GANG**